Children's Rules

BY PAULA GROOTHUIS

Legwork Team
Publishing
NEW YORK

Legwork Team Publishing
New York
631-398-2004
www.legworkteam.com

Disclaimer: This book, intended for young readers, is for educational and entertainment purposes only.

First Edition: 02/20/2018

Printed in the United States of America
This book is printed on acid-free paper

To my children and grandchildren
and to parents who handle their children
in a loving way.

ACKNOWLEDGMENTS

I would like to acknowledge a friend, Carol Forster, who encouraged me to read about parenting and to take a workshop back in the 1970s. I am grateful for the authors of the books: Chaim Ginott, Adele Faber, and Elaine Mazlish, and in addition, to all that I learned in the class. I could not be more proud of who my children are today and how they parent their own children.

INTRODUCTION

Back in the 1970s when I was raising a toddler, I sometimes got frustrated with the way I spoke to her, this child that I loved. Children sometimes need discipline, but I learned by reading and taking a class how to handle discipline in a logical way that would teach my children, not make them feel angry or frustrated, even though I was frustrated. Wanting all parental relationships to be as positive as possible has motivated me to get these thoughts out. I hope this book can reach out to children to know they are loved and can help them understand the right actions and reactions in their behavior.

Our parents at home and our teachers at schools
Teach us, the kids, lots of rules.
As children, we listen to what our parents and teachers say.
They are helping us to live in a kind, loving, and caring way!

We learn about eating to stay healthy and strong.
We don't want to stuff ourselves with food they say is wrong.
We eat breakfast in the morning and dinner at night.
We learn how to eat and take a careful bite.

We have our lunch right around noon
And learn to eat with a fork and a spoon.
We eat three meals every day;
From a sharp knife we keep our hands away.

Not too much sugar, not too much dessert,
We try to stay clean, without food on our shirt.

In a restaurant as we take each bite,
We use a quiet voice and remain seated to be polite.

Also, at home when we eat,
Until the family is done, we stay in our seat.

When we talk in different places we
make a good choice,
To be aware of using a loud or a quiet voice.
At certain fun places like the playground,
We can use a loud voice and run all around.

That outside voice is fine when we're playing outdoors and having fun.
The inside voice is the quiet one.
To be used in the library, a restaurant, a control we must keep,
And at home we try not to make a peep
When someone nearby is falling asleep.

We are being polite by saying "Thank you" and "Please",
"Bless you" too when we hear someone sneeze.

AAA-
CHOO!!

We hold our parents' hands as streets are being crossed.
We want to be careful and not get hurt or lost.
In the parking lot as well, while we're not going too far,
We want to be safe from any moving car.

While in our cars, we make sure
That we are always safe and secure.
When we're going for a ride down any street,
We put on a seat belt and stay in our car seat.

It's fun to play with toys every day.

When we're finished it's time to put them away.

They may go in boxes or up on shelves,

And we can put them away all by ourselves.

Some small toys may go in a drawer,

And we can pretend to be a vacuum cleaner and get them off the floor.

Yes, playing with toys is such a treat,

And we can keep things clean and neat.

Because they're organized they'll be easily found;

Then later we'll again have a good time playing around.

If we are asked to help around the house once in a while,
Our support will make our family smile.
We can help wash and fold our clothes,
Water flowers and the lawn with a hose.
And after we eat and drink,
We can walk our dishes to the sink.
We can learn to cook and bake.
Our bed we can even help to make.

VACUUM-CLEANING

WASHING DISHES

WATER THE FLOWERS

LAUNDRY

We also have some body cleaning plans.
We wash our face, and we wash our hands.
Our teeth we get to brush.
The toilet we learn to flush.
We take a shower or a bath,
It all leads us on a healthy path.

Sometimes there are difficult situations, in which we deal,
But hands are not for hitting, no matter how angry we feel.
Instead, we use our words to explain;
That is why we have a brain.
We express ourselves to let someone know
We can control how things will go.
We look into our brain, our thoughts to find—
Helpful words to express what is on our mind.
Using our words to handle a fight is a much better way
Because we can think about what we should say.
For the way we respond, we have a choice:
To control our tone and use a kind, calm voice.

If someone is making a fuss
And is not nice to us,
We may think they are being rude
But maybe they are in a bad mood.
Often we will find
It helps them more when we are kind.

They may not have a happy soul,
So we can help them to feel more whole!

There may be some toys we do not want to share.
We can find some for our friends to use, to show we care.

And when we go off to school
We all pay attention to each rule.
To ask and answer a question, a hand goes up in the air.
We follow directions and stay in our chair.
In the classroom we learn to listen through the years.
That is why we have our ears.

We don't always get what we want: what we're wishing for.
We may want something but we can't have more.
Mom and Dad may say it's time to go,
And we're not quite ready though.
We can't always have things going our way.
It may or may not be a toy-buying day.
Our parents do have to say "no" at times, and it's not to make us cry;
They have a good reason though we may not know why.
Sometimes there are things we have to do
Even though as a child, we don't have the same view.
We should also listen to get ready for bed at night,
And do what our parents say is right.
There are lots of reasons why,
So we should always do our best to try.

Our parents are there to give us a hand,
Even when we are angry, we can try to understand.
To make us happy is their goal
To bring us up to feel confident and whole.

We want our thumbs up, not down,
And a smile on our face, not a frown.

To do the things we love to do,
To have a positive optimistic view,
To be respectful and respected, to be proud as can be
To love the world around and to be able to say, "I love me!"

We have learned so much from this book so far:
To eat healthy and how to sit in a car,
To express what is on our mind,
To get out our anger but still be considerate and kind,
To take our parents', teachers', and families' advice,
To be thoughtful, careful, helpful, and nice,
When to be quiet and when to be loud,
Of ourselves we will always be proud,
To never use our hands to hit,
To all good things we will commit,
Not to get in a physical fight,
To listen, stay safe, be respectful, and polite,
To share our toys and then put them away,
To have fun, try our best and be happy every day!
From the love around us, we can learn what's right, not wrong,
For all of us on our planet to have peace and get along!

NOTES TO PARENTS AND TEACHERS IN RHYME

Let's think about how to bring up our children today:
Using calm, uplifting advice in a special way,
If we express ourselves with anger and frustration and always make a fuss,
They may start to act just like us.
While we do get angry at them and get annoyed,
There are certain automatic reactions we should try to avoid.
There are definitely ways to express each rule
Without sounding angry, bossy, or cruel
To parent and teach well, we can follow some rules,
From workshops and reading books, here are some suggested tools:
It is a helpful tool to "**Mirror their Feelings**"
To deal with many situations, emotional reactions, daily dealings,
While their frustration and disappointments are being expressed,
Our understanding can help them be less stressed.
"**Granting in fantasy what you can't have in reality**" can put us all on fire;
It helps kids know we want to help with their desire.
While they may not feel it's going so good,
It shows on some level that we as parents understood.
To solve issues and problems to get through the day,
Giving them choices is another way.
It encourages independence and keeps things light—
It also helps them learn what is right.
If they do refuse to make our choice,
We can tell them what should be done using a quiet patient voice.
Sometimes depending what is going on, it can be nice,
Just to listen to our children instead of always giving advice.
Through the years we can see a positive result,
Which will have a positive effect as they each become an adult.

NOTES TO PARENTS AND TEACHERS IN PROSE

I not only want to hopefully motivate our children to follow our rules, I would like to share some parenting and teaching thoughts. Even though there may have been a reason to be frustrated, there I was reacting to those that I cared about in a way that didn't feel right. I don't want any parent or teacher to feel guilty but to see the paradox between the intense love we feel for our precious children and the everyday messages they may receive. If we all treated them with respect and communicated in an upbeat positive way, couldn't that be like a little pebble thrown into a body of water with a rippling effect that could affect the entire family, the community, the world? As a teacher, when children were misbehaving, instead of drawing attention to their behavior, I praised those that were behaving and it often turned the others around in a positive way. And many books and workshops that we can all expose ourselves to can help us in raising our children and teaching others. When I did not like the way I sometimes spoke to my children who I loved more than anything in the world, I started to learn what I call new tools to handle different frustrating situations. What a difference that made in my everyday life dealing with bringing up my children to be who they are today. At this point, they are responsible adults with self-esteem and I am so proud of them both and love the way they are bringing up their children. I had learned to **mirror their feelings, grant in fantasy what they could not have in reality, give them choices** and just consistently respond in logical supportive solution-oriented ways through the years that I feel have helped them be who they are today.

ABOUT THE AUTHOR

Paula Groothuis is a speech therapist, an author, and rhymer who lives on Long Island. She is the mother of two grown children who are successful and have been well educated through the years. As a speech therapist, mother and now a grandmother, she has been inspired to write this book to continue to reach out to children in an effort to help them live in a kind, loving, and caring way!

Children's Rules

For more information regarding Paula Groothuis and her work,
visit her website: www.PersonalizedPoemsByPaula.com

Further copies of this book may be purchased online from
LegworkTeam.com; Amazon.com; BarnesandNoble.com or
via the author's website, www.PersonalizedPoemsByPaula.com

You can also obtain a copy by ordering it from your favorite bookstore.

CPSIA information can be obtained
at www.ICGtesting.com
Printed in the USA
BVHW02s0351280418
514691BV00005B/5/P